D0285419

Also by Andy Borowitz

The Trillionaire Next Door

Rationalizations to Live By
(with Henry Beard and John Boswell)

Who Moved My Soap?

The CEO's Guide to Surviving in Prison

Andy Borowitz

SIMON & SCHUSTER

NEW YORK   LONDON   TORONTO   SYDNEY   SINGAPORE

SIMON & SCHUSTER
Rockefeller Center
1230 Avenue of the Americas
New York, NY 10020

This book is a work of fiction. Names, characters, places,
and incidents either are products of the author's imagination
or are used fictitiously. Any resemblance to actual events or
locales or persons, living or dead, is entirely coincidental.

Copyright © 2003 by Andy Borowitz

All rights reserved,
including the right of reproduction
in whole or in part in any form.

First Simon & Schuster trade paperback edition 2003

SIMON & SCHUSTER and colophon are
registered trademarks of Simon & Schuster, Inc.

For information about special discounts for bulk purchases,
please contact Simon & Schuster Special Sales:
1-800-456-6798 or business@simonandschuster.com

Illustrations © Michael Kupperman

Designed by Karolina Harris

Manufactured in the United States of America

10 9 8 7 6 5 4 3 2

Library of Congress Cataloging-in-Publication Data
Borowitz, Andy.
Who moved my soap? : the CEO's guide to surviving
in prison / Andy Borowitz
p.   cm
ISBN 0-7432-5142-3
1. Prisoners—United States—Humor. 2. Executives—
Professional ethics—United States—Humor. I. Title.
HV9471.B67 2003
365'.6'0207—dc21

2003045731

TABLE OF CONTENTS

1. Put Your Hands in the Air and Step Away from the Desk _1_

2. From the Big Board to the Big House _6_

3. Trading One Gated Community for Another _15_

4. Packing for the Pokey _24_

5. Prison Slang: From Ass-out to Zip Gun _31_

6. Prison Food: Don't Pick Up the Check _38_

7. The Seven Habits of Highly Effective Prisoners™ _46_

8. Prison Cell Feng Shui _60_

9. Bringing Six Sigma to Sing Sing _64_

10. Female CEOs: Breaking Through the Concrete Ceiling _70_

11. How Golden Is Your Hacksaw? Exit Strategies _78_

Put Your Hands in the Air and Step Away from the Desk

If you're a convicted CEO who's heading to prison for the first time, let me just say this: You should be totally stoked. A trip to the slammer could be the best career move you ever made, and after a few weeks behind bars, you'll be kicking yourself for not getting convicted sooner.

Surprised? I thought you might be. You've probably bought into the conventional wisdom that a prison sentence is some kind of "punishment," a fate to be avoided at all costs. Well, you won't see me slicing that brand of baloney. If you follow the simple advice in this book, you'll discover what successful CEO convicts everywhere already know: If time is money, then hard time is hard cash.

Are you drinking the Kool-Aid yet? If not, perhaps a few facts will change your mind:

Thanks to the rising tide of corporate scandals, former CEOs are pouring into America's penitentiaries in record numbers, the biggest migration of white-collar criminals into the penal system since the fall of the Nixon administration. Within the next five years, one out of four CEOs in the United States will be convicted and sent to jail, while another one out of four will flee the country in a single-engine plane with gold coins and priceless diamonds sewn into his underpants. Still another one out of four will plea-bargain his way into performing community service, such as teaching inner city youths and the elderly how to destroy incriminating documents and create fictitious off-the-books partnerships.

But that still leaves a whole lot of CEOs heading up the river—good news for you, because you'll be far from alone. Once you're in prison, if you look to your right, and then to your left, your chances of recognizing someone from your business school class will be better than 50 percent, and even better than that if you went to Harvard. According to a recent study, prison construction in the United States is lagging well behind the pace of CEO convictions, and by the end of the decade there will be as many as *one hundred thousand* CEOs behind bars—roughly ten thousand times the number of people who are looking forward to the next Meg Ryan film.

Will prison change these chief executive offenders? Based on anecdotal evidence, just the opposite is occurring. With each passing day, these "barbarians at the prison gate" are reinventing prison as we know it, turning up their noses at such outmoded goals of incarceration as "rehabilitation" and "paying one's debt to society." Being thrown in a cell hasn't kept them from thinking outside the box—far from it. When an incarcerated CEO wakes up in the morning, he doesn't see the concrete walls, the barbed wire, or the ferocious guard dogs—he sees an ideal place to grow a new business, far from the prying eyes of the SEC and the Department of Justice. The inmate of yesteryear was always looking for a fight; today's convicted CEO is in search of excellence.

So before you head off to the pokey, get over that shopworn myth about prison being a bad thing. If you're smart enough and savvy enough—and the fact that you've bought this book is a pretty good sign that you are both—you'll emerge from your time in the joint more productive, more innovative, and millions of dollars wealthier than you were on the day that the prison guard first checked you for lice.

Not buying this? I know what you're thinking: I'm just another slick con man, primed to sell you a bill of goods and make out like a bandit.

Well, guess again: I'm a convicted CEO myself.

That's right. And I'm not just some run-of-the-mill, caught-with-his-hands-in-the-cookie-jar CEO, either: Just last year, *Forbes* named me one of "America's Top

100 Convicted CEOs," putting my police mug shot on the cover of that esteemed publication. Yes, *Forbes* gave me my "props," and in the select fraternity of imprisoned chief executives, it doesn't get any better than that.

I can tell you still have your doubts. "If he's so important," you say, your words slurred by the cocktail of antidepressants and tranquilizers you've been on ever since your verdict was announced, "why did he even bother to write this book?" A good question that deserves a good answer—and this time, for a change, I won't take the Fifth.

Before I took my first fateful ride on the so-called "dog bus" to prison, shackled to a fellow convict who had a picture of the cast of "The Facts of Life" tattooed on his back, I paid a visit to my local bookstore, hoping to find some reference work that might help ease my transition from CEO to CBO (Cell Block Occupant). What did I find there? Cookbooks. Cat books. Book after book of poetry by the pop singer Jewel, all drastically reduced. But nowhere did I find a book preparing the former CEO for his stay in prison, even though convicted CEOs represent the fastest-growing segment of the reading public today. I vowed with all my heart to correct this sad state of affairs, and once I received assurances from my attorney that the thousands of shareholders currently engaged in class-action lawsuits against me could claim no share of my publishing royalties, I buckled down and began to write.

Writing a book while in prison is not an easy task. When an inmate in the cell next to mine started screaming, "Press the bunk, punk!!!" at the top of his lungs, I could not ask him to keep it down; when I dropped my pen on the floor, I was afraid to pick it up. Yet, somehow, I prevailed, and you are now holding the fruits of my efforts in your sweaty, trembling hands.

If you're a CEO who's been caught, this is the one book you won't want to be caught without. I hope this book is helpful as you trade your pinstripes for horizontal ones. I hope this book is long enough to answer your most pressing questions, short enough to hold your attention, yet thick enough to hollow out and hide a small weapon in. Read it, study it, learn from it—and for heaven's sake, don't skim it. After all, you're not going anywhere.

U.S. Penitentiary Lomax, Cell Block Six
Lomax, Alabama
January 2003

From the Big Board
to the Big House

Here's a little quiz. Who said this: "I'm innocent, man. I was framed. And if anybody says otherwise, I'll kick his ass."

If you guessed Kenneth Lay, the former CEO of Enron, that's a good guess—but you're off by a mile.

It was actually said to me by my cell mate, a career criminal named Snake (not his real name). Snake, who has the powerful, muscular build of a younger Arnold

Schwarzenegger and the hard, don't-mess-with-me fa-
cial features of an older Joan Collins, proclaimed his innocence the first day I arrived in Cell Block Six, and he
rarely misses an opportunity to reproclaim it; in fact,
Snake talks about his innocence almost as much as
CEOs talk about their severance packages. To hear him
tell it, Snake has been framed for a remarkable string of
car thefts, armed robberies, and assorted other felonies
going back twenty years. When I asked him who, exactly, would have had a vested interest in framing him
for these crimes, Snake looked at me as if I were an idiot
and said, simply, "A woman named Faye Resnick." I
thought it best not to explore the matter further.

Snake is not alone in complaining that the criminal
justice system has treated him unfairly. Nearly every
prisoner I've encountered since I came here vehemently
protests his innocence and takes absolutely no personal
responsibility for having wound up behind bars. When I
hear them go on in this vein (and they do go on), I must
admit that I feel very much alone—because unlike them,
I really am innocent, and it's not my fault that I'm in
here.

You're probably familiar with the unfortunate chain of
events that led me to Cell Block Six, unless you've been
too busy fleeing from the authorities to read a newspaper. No other recent business scandal has eclipsed the
spectacular collapse and bankruptcy of the company I
headed, the energy-telecom-pharmaceutical giant called
Shamco International. I'm not one to dredge up ancient
history, nor do I enjoy rehashing a story in which I have
repeatedly and unjustly been cast in the role of scum-
bag. However, since the credibility of this book depends

wholly on the credibility of its author, I feel obliged to tell you my side of the story, which, by the way, also happens to be the truth—regardless of what my jury unanimously thought.

Founded in 1997 by me and my then–business partner, the world-renowned fugitive financier Viktor M. Saurian, Shamco was a conglomeration of three smaller companies—KleptoCom, Larcenex, and Fungible Data—that Viktor and I acquired through a complex series of stock transactions, arbitrage plays, and one very successful bake sale. Making the disparate cultures of those three companies mesh was no small feat, especially since one of them, KleptoCom, turned out not to exist at all. It was rough going at first, and Viktor and I were forced to slash payroll and overhead, eventually moving our offices from a former Arthur Treacher's Fish 'n' Chips restaurant in Dayton, Ohio, to a twenty-four-hour photo booth in the middle of a CVS parking lot. But before you could say "Dow 30,000," all of our hard work paid off in spades: Shamco became one of the high-flying momentum stocks of the late 1990s, even dwarfing such then-hot Wall Street darlings as tubesocksbymail.com and 1-800-CATFOOD.

Flush with paper wealth, we moved our corporate headquarters from Dayton to the Las Vegas Strip and went on an acquisitions binge, investing in such far-flung businesses as genetically engineered cow manure and Liza Minnelli's marriage. Growing like a pesticide-resistant weed, Shamco eventually came to acquire twenty more companies and six U.S. senators. Suddenly, Viktor and I became feared, envied, and sexually attractive. As our company's stock price rocketed to increasingly empyreal heights, I had to pinch myself so often that I eventually hired a Stanford MBA whose only job was to pinch me, freeing me up for more pressing tasks like strategic planning and going to antique car auctions.

But, as a wise man once said, "Nothing lasts forever"—and Shamco, sad to say, was one of those nothings that didn't.

I'll never forget the day when our magnificent company, this towering monument to our hard work and other people's money, came a-tumbling down like a house of maxed-out MasterCards.

I was on the Isle of Capri throwing a gala birthday celebration for my new bride, Conspicuosa von Mammon, a former Miss Benelux whom Viktor and I had met just two weeks earlier when she brought nachos to our table at our favorite restaurant near the Shamco corporate campus, Señor Wiggles Grill and Bar. I won't go into lengthy details about our courtship, because there aren't any: The moment I saw Conspicuosa, I fell wildly, madly in love for the first time in my life. One week later, she became my third wife.

On the weekend that Conspicuosa turned twenty-six, I flew two thousand of Shamco's senior vice presidents to Capri where, for forty-eight hours, they drank, tanned, drank some more, had complimentary Botox injections, and chowed down on a lip-smacking array of gourmet delicacies, including super-spicy "hot hot hot wings" at a food station manned by none other than Queen Elizabeth II. (She doesn't do many corporate events, but she's available, so long as you're willing to pay her appearance fee and her hefty room service bill—apparently, the lady goes through Toblerones like she hasn't eaten in a year.) Naked footmen, their glistening bodies painted with two coats of genuine 24K platinum, waited on my inebriated executives hand and foot. A ten-foot-tall ice sculpture rendering of Eduard Munch's *The Scream* spewed Cristal champagne from its gaping, horrifying mouth. The party, in a word, ruled.

But as Sunday night drew to a close and the best and the brightest of Shamco International sang an unforgettable rendition of "Happy Birthday" to Conspicuosa— led by Celine Dion, Luciano Pavarotti, and several key members of the Goo Goo Dolls—I got a call on my cell phone that would change my life forever.

"This is the SEC," the voice on the other end said.

"Sexy who?" I shouted, straining to hear over Pavarotti's ear-splitting high A.

"The SEC. We'd like to ask you a few questions."

Snapping out of my Cristal-fueled mellow, I immediately referred the caller to our general counsel, who at that very moment was dancing the Lambada ("The Forbidden Dance") with magician David Blaine, a late addition to the weekend's swollen entertainment roster. Heaving my phone into the blazing luau-style bonfire, I dashed away and boarded the Shamco corporate Concorde, flying back to Vegas faster than Wayne Newton with a second mortgage to pay.

Minutes after the plane touched down in Nevada, my limo driver, Kato, whisked me off to the Shamco campus, where I immediately started feeding seventeen thousand pages of highly sensitive financial documents into a custom-built nuclear-powered paper shredder I'd bought for situations just like this. Its inventor, a former

Microsoft genius who'd been exiled from Redmond when he made fun of the shape of Steven Ballmer's head, had promised me that this technological marvel could eat the Shanghai phone book in 4.3 seconds, a new world record.

He wasn't blowing smoke up my ass. Just moments after I powered up its miniature reactor, the shredder devoured fiscal 1998, 1999, and 2000 in great, awful gulps. It also made short work of a highly damaging letter we had just received from the FDA, rejecting our anti-baldness drug Follicure on the grounds that it not only failed to cause hair to grow but it also caused side effects alarmingly reminiscent of Tourette's syndrome. It swallowed whole a damning memo from our CFO to the headmaster of an exclusive Las Vegas preschool, in which our CFO promised that Shamco would finance a martial arts–themed Broadway musical starring the headmaster himself in exchange for preschool admission for the CFO's quadruplets. But then, with a horrible *whoosh* I shall never forget, the machine sucked the sleeve of my Kenneth Cole tuxedo shirt into its ravenous maw, its piranha-like jaws closing and refusing to let me go. It was upon this seemingly incriminating tableau that twenty-seven FBI agents barged into the room, capturing the whole fiasco on video—footage that proved less than helpful during the sentencing phase of my trial.

I'd be surprised if you didn't see my so-called "perp walk," since it was carried live by every major cable network in the country including CNN, CNBC, and, for reasons that are still not entirely clear to me, the Weather Channel. Only two days after that infernal shredder tried to take my arm off, the Department of

Justice threw 1,702 separate indictments at me, a new high-water mark for politically motivated prosecutorial overkill. Just twelve months earlier, *Business Week* had hailed me as a capitalist visionary who was reinventing the American corporate landscape; now I had mutated monstrously into a convenient scapegoat for a suddenly souring economy. Yes, I was an easy mark, someone to take the heat off the true culprits: Mr. Alan Greenspan and his inept cadre of economic do-nothings in Washington, D.C., empty suits who fiddled while the Dow and the NASDAQ burned.

Three burly Justice Department goons led me away in handcuffs from my home in the exclusive gated community of Xanadu Estates while my beloved wife, Conspicuosa, who had been rudely rousted during a leg-waxing appointment, looked on as bravely as she could, tears falling from her cheeks and splashing onto her Manolo Blahnik sling backs. Our 87,000-square-foot home, containing such custom-made conveniences as a $19,000 bathroom scale and an emerald-encrusted VCR remote, soon became predictable fodder for the vicious, puerile jesting of Jay Leno, David Letterman, and a jeering Greek chorus of TV talking heads. In a typically scolding editorial, the *New York Times* called the Shamco affair "the single biggest swindle perpetrated on the American public since the movie *Scooby-Doo* was released." By the end of that week, my *Weekus horribilus,* twenty thousand separate shareholder lawsuits had been filed against me, our company's logo had been removed from the major league baseball stadium Shamco Field, and Mick Jagger, once my dearest friend, was no longer returning my phone calls, even when I disguised my voice to sound like a Brazilian supermodel.

I won't recount the details of that orgy of name-calling and finger-pointing that the press disingenuously referred to as my "trial." But there is one fact that seemed to have gotten lost in the media-driven rush to judgment. My decision to drain our company's pension fund to buy that mansion in Xanadu Estates was made with one and only one person in mind: John Q. Shareholder.

What the jury at my trial failed to grasp is that it is the fiduciary obligation of every CEO to maintain a high-end lifestyle for the good of his company. Living like a pasha is the only way a CEO can effectively convey the message to Wall Street that his company is prospering and worthy of the investment community's continuing confidence. If I had neglected this responsibility and lived in a more modest dwelling—say, a 6,000-square-foot ranch house with a normal bathroom scale and remote—every securities analyst who covered Shamco would have taken that as a sign that all was not well with the company's balance sheet. Faster than you can say "company officials were not available for comment," these very same analysts would have unsheathed their merciless swords on *Lou Dobbs' Moneyline,* shaving billions off our company's market cap in a matter of milliseconds. To prevent that from happening, I lived up to my fiduciary responsibility the best way I knew how: by moving with my wife into the largest mansion we could find in the state of Nevada. And what was our reward? For me, a one-way ticket to the clink, and for Conspicuosa, an even worse sentence: being forced to live alone in an 87,000-square-foot—yes, let's call it a prison—with nobody but a twenty-five-member household staff and her tennis pro, Chad, to keep her company.

To any former Shamco shareholders who may be reading these words, let me say this: If my real crime was caring too much about your financial well-being and doing everything in my power to preserve the value of your Shamco shares and 401(k) accounts, then I stand before you today, guilty as charged. I realize that for some of you, that confession may fall short of what you were looking for—but I can assure you, it's from the heart.

Even though I did nothing wrong, knowing that hundreds of thousands of Shamco investors lost $34.6 billion of their hard-earned money is something that will haunt me for the rest of my life and fill my every waking moment with sadness and regret. As corny as this may sound, I hope that writing this book will, in some small way, help make amends. To that end, I would like to offer each and every former shareholder of Shamco the exclusive opportunity to buy this book from me at a special "shareholder's discount," in exchange for dropping any and all lawsuits against me. I hope this offer will, in some small way, get the healing process rolling, and I will be happy to throw in free shipping for all orders of ten books or more.

3

Trading One Gated Community for Another

At least once a week I'll get a phone call from another former Shamco associate who wants to know what prison is really like. My answer is always the same: "Oh, you'll find out soon enough." This wisecrack usually results in dead silence on the other end of the line and a quick hang-up, but as an inveterate practical jokester I just can't resist saying it. I guess some prisoners lose their sense of humor behind bars, but not me—it's one of the things that keep me going.

As a recently convicted CEO, you, too, are probably wondering what prison is really like—and you may also be wondering what makes me such an authority on the subject. Sure, I've told you that I'm writing this book from prison, but you're probably not picturing me in a *prison* prison. I'll bet you think I'm lolling about in one of those so-called "country club" prisons like the legendary "Club Fed," sipping from a tumbler of Chivas while I lazily dictate this book to some high-priced ghostwriter like Norman Mailer or Joan Didion or whoever wrote Charles Barkley's book. You're probably picturing a place where the harshest punishment is having your DSL service cut off for the afternoon and where the prisoners only riot when the mess hall runs out of Beluga.

Well, permit me to drop a bomb on you: For the past six months, I've been doing time at the United States Penitentiary in Lomax, Alabama, a maximum security facility that *Consumer Reports* has consistently rated as "America's Worst Place to Be Locked Up In." You see, when those political opportunists at the so-called Department of Justice decided to make an example of me, they didn't pull any punches. Believe me, there's no golf course at Lomax, and when someone picks up a club, you run like hell. And riots? Last week we had a real barnburner that erupted when two prisoners got into an argument over who played the character Screech on *Saved by the Bell.* While no prisoners were beaten to an unrecognizable pulp in the spiraling brawl, several were beaten to a recognizable one, which, from where I sit, is just about as bad. All in all, if you think the shareholders at your last annual meeting were on a short fuse, you haven't been to Lomax.

I mention these details only to establish my authority, and not to paint an unduly scary picture of prison life. That, it seems, is Hollywood's job. Movies like *The Green Mile* and television programs like *Oz* have wildly distorted the prison experience in the name of entertainment, just as the film *The Sound of Music* recklessly exaggerated the singing talents of the average nun. According to Hollywood, the minute you're behind bars you're served meals unfit for a tree-shrew, forced at knifepoint to wear a "doo rag" on your head, and harassed by fellow convicts with biceps like HoneyBaked Hams and all the self-control of a pack of South Florida State sorority sisters in a *Girls Gone Wild* video.

How accurate is this so-called Hollywood version of prison life? Maybe it's time for a reality check. In the six months since I came to Lomax, have I once been required to eat repellent food, been made to wear unflattering headgear, or been bullied by bands of vicious sociopaths?

To be honest, all three of those things have happened to me at Lomax. In fact, they all happened on my first day here, a day I'm not likely to forget any time soon. Since that day, those three things continued to happen to me with startling regularity, again and again and again. If there's any lesson in this, I suppose, it's that even Hollywood, with its wildly stereotyped portrayals of prison life, gets things right every now and then.

As your first day behind bars approaches, your imagination may become fertile ground for a wide variety of nightmare scenarios. You may find it difficult to sleep at night and may derive little or no pleasure from activities you usually enjoy, like torching a document storage warehouse or burying your hard drive in a landfill. The imminent prospect of confinement may fill you with terrible feelings of claustrophobia, reminding you of the time that bonehead in your travel department forgot to fuel up your company jet and you were forced to fly first class on Delta instead. You may fret that being imprisoned for fraud and embezzlement will affect the way the outside world regards you and might even hurt your chances of running another Fortune 500 company someday. And you may privately worry that the executive committee of your yacht club didn't really buy your story that you were suspending your membership because you intended to spend the next five to ten years visiting America's most historic hockey arenas.

Once again, it's time for a reality check. For starters, let's take a look at the issue of "confinement."

If I described to you a person who spent all day cooped up in one room and was never free to come and go as he pleased, I'd be talking about the average prisoner in a federal penitentiary, right?

Wrong: I'd be describing the average CEO.

Think about it: How many times in the past five years did you tell someone that you couldn't see him or her because you were "tied up" in meetings all day? How many times did you cancel anniversary dinners with your wife or visits to your mother in her assisted-living facility because you were "stuck in the office" or "chained to your desk" and couldn't "escape"? The more you look at your old CEO lifestyle, the more confining and "prison-like" it seems—which, when you stop and think about it, is really pretty ironic.

In marked contrast with the cramped, hemmed-in life of a CEO, a prisoner's existence is the very opposite of confining. In prison, you're rarely in one place for very long—not if you know what's good for you. Between the guards shouting "Bump it on down, peckerwood!" and your fellow prisoners coming at you with "shivs" and "shanks," every day in prison quickly turns into a high-impact aerobic workout that would make an Olympic pentathlete cry uncle. Running, ducking, dodging fists and zip guns—the prison lifestyle is the most active lifestyle there is. I'm not a betting man, but I'm willing to wager that you'll emerge from your time behind bars with well-defined pecs, rock-hard abs, and long, lean muscles that will make you the envy of all those corporate fat-asses you used to work with.

How did the myth about prison being "confining" get started in the first place? No one knows for sure, but maybe it stemmed from the old saying that a prison cell is so tiny, "there's not enough room to swing a dead cat in it." Speaking from my experience, nothing could be farther from the truth. Not only does a prison cell have enough room to swing a dead cat in it, it has more than enough room to swing a tire iron in it, as my cell mate Snake has proved time and time again.

What about that other tired old canard about prison life—that inmates suffer the hardship of isolation, being separated from friends and loved ones for long periods of time? There's a grain of truth to this, but only a grain. True, as a prisoner, you'll see your family only once a month—but that's probably once a month more than you saw them when you were a CEO. As for other relatives, like that no-account brother-in-law of yours who keeps hitting you up for cash to start his own barnyard-animal porn site, you'll come to appreciate and even cherish that thick pane of glass that separates you from him. Prisoners, you see, have the unique opportunity to put family members on "mute"—a luxury that so-called "free" people can only dream of. This is why, in my view, CEOs who instruct their attorneys to beg and plead for so-called "house arrest" rather than for a traditional prison sentence are really missing the boat. If you're going to be locked up for an extended period of time, it's infinitely better to be locked up away from relatives than with them.

Now what about that other nagging concern of yours: that being in prison will somehow adversely affect how you are perceived by the outside world? That worry, as it turns out, is pretty stupid, too.

It is true that the reputation of convicted CEOs took it on the chin over the last year or so; in 2002, in fact, CEOs briefly replaced lawyers as the most common butts of lame jokes circulated on the Internet. But that trend appears to have been short-lived, since by year's end both CEOs and lawyers had been supplanted in such jokes by members of the clergy. Today, the public's regard for convicted CEOs seems to be on the rebound. In fact, I would argue that far from being the social stigma many former CEOs fear it to be, a prison sentence may actually be the newest and truest status symbol in corporate America today. And unlike such ephemeral status symbols as a corner office or a fancy title, a prison sentence is something that endures, sometimes for twenty years or more, and sometimes forever.

Why is going to prison the ultimate sign that you've arrived? It's a simple matter of logic. Government prosecutors, in their relentless search for the next headline-grabbing "perp walk," only want to reel in the biggest fish—so the very fact that you were arrested, hand-cuffed, and eventually convicted of a felony is the ulti-mate proof of just how big a fish you are. If you were found guilty of hundreds of felonies, as I was, that's even more prestigious.

Think about it. When was the last time you saw some-one from middle management paraded in front of TV cameras? The answer, of course, is never. Middle man-agement drones, with their puny stock options, pathetic per diems, and factory-financed Nissan Sentras are the little fish of the corporate world. They're destined to lead lives of quiet desperation, haunted by the knowledge that their chances of ever receiving a high-profile prison sen-tence like the one you just got are somewhere between slim and none. Going to prison, it turns out, isn't a fate to be avoided at all costs—but not going just might be.

It's a widely overlooked fact that the unluckiest CEOs of the past few years weren't the ones who went to prison, but rather the ones who, quite literally, "couldn't get arrested." Case in point: "Neutron Jack" Welch, the former CEO of General Electric.

During his tenure as the GE chief, Jack Welch became the most celebrated CEO of his day, multiplying his company's market cap many times over, dominating several global industries, and even acquiring the NBC television network, home to such popular programming as *Friends* and the three dozen *Law and Order* spin-offs. Yes, at GE, Jack Welch truly did "bring good things to life"—and what was his reward? Humiliating tab-loid headlines about his generous retirement perks and his affair with a *Harvard Business Review* editor, Suzy

Wetlaufer. On the other hand, if Welch had gone to prison instead of into retirement, it would have been a whole different story. If Neutron Jack had become New Jack, there would have been no outrageous perks for the press to have a field day with, and any randy dalliances he had behind bars would have been his own little secret. Yes, life would have been sweet for Mr. Welch if only he'd been thrown in the slammer—but since he neglected to commit any felonies while he was CEO, it just wasn't to be.

Going to prison, then, confers many benefits on the prisoner—but is this really such a new development? Hardly. For many of the greatest figures in world history, their time behind bars was the one and only thing that really put them on the map.

Consider, if you will, the Marquis de Sade (1740– 1814). Before he was incarcerated, the marquis was an obscure aristocrat with a fondness for whips and nipple clamps who seemed destined for the oblivion of history's dustbin. But going to prison changed all that. Today, he is the inspiration for an entire branch of sexual deviancy, as well as for many exclusive, well-attended nightclubs in New York, London, and other world capitals. In contrast with the Marquis de Sade, the pop singer Sade (1959–) never went to prison, and hasn't been heard from much since her early hits "Smooth Operator" and "No Ordinary Love." How would you rather be remembered? As far as I'm concerned, it's not even close.

I would be negligent if I detailed the perks of going to prison without mentioning prison's greatest gift of all to the convicted CEO: the gift of time. Remember how many times you told yourself, back when you were a free man, "If only I could take a year off, I'd finally read all the great books—*War and Peace, Madame Bovary,* and *Remembrance of Things Past?*" Well, multiply that year by five, ten, or, in my case, thirty-five. In prison you'll have more than enough time to read—if not those three books, then the thousands of stained, marked-up, pages-missing old paperbacks that line the shelves of most prison libraries.

Go ahead and say it: sweet.

Packing for the Pokey

If you swallowed the last chapter whole, you've probably shed most of your fears about going to prison by now and are actually getting pretty jazzed about the whole deal. You're still losing sleep, of course, but not out of anxiety—rather, from the sheer anticipation of what lies ahead. Even that ugly prison uniform, which you used to dread putting on, now seems a whole lot more flattering than most of the golf pants you own. Remember how excited you were at the beginning of your corporate career when you stole that junior VP title right out from under your best friend from B-school and sent him into a downward career spiral from which he never fully recovered? As great a feeling as that was, it's not even close to how stoked you feel right now.

As you count down the days until your prison sentence begins, you may feel your body tingling with excitement like a rosy-cheeked debutante getting ready for her first cotillion. These are perfectly normal feelings to have before you go to prison, and many prisoners continue to have such feelings long after they are incarcerated. But let's not get ahead of ourselves. Before you even get to prison, you have a much more immediate challenge to face: how to pack.

If you ask most repeat offenders what's the most important thing for a prisoner to pack, they're likely to give you a one-word answer: "Heat." By this, of course, they mean firearms, and who can blame them? It's only natural to want to bring a gun with you when you're going to prison, a place that's literally "swimming with sharks." For any of you who might be harboring fantasies of smuggling a weapon into prison, however, I should warn you that most CEOs would stand a better chance of passing a scientifically administered lie detector test. You shouldn't even try to smuggle in weapons, for two reasons. First, all federal penitentiaries are outfitted with metal detectors, making any attempt to sneak a weapon into the facility doomed to failure; and second, such a risky endeavor is entirely unnecessary, since weapons of every kind imaginable are cheap, plentiful, and readily available once you're behind bars.

Which brings us back to our original question: If you're not packing heat, what should you pack?

Jimmy "Jimbo" Pelson is a name that should be familiar to many of you. Jimbo made some pretty ugly headlines back in 2001 when he was CEO of the health-care giant Benevola, which cratered when the government discovered that it had been listing all of its expenses on its balance sheet in disappearing ink. The feds were already investigating Jimbo's expenditure of $110 million, officially listed in the Benevola annual report as the line item "Band-Aids," to finance his purchase of a beach villa in Cannes that had once been owned by the emperor Charlemagne. Things went from bad to worse for Jimbo at his fraud trial when he claimed that he had somehow lost $4.6 billion from the company's pension fund "down a grate." I had met Jimbo a few months earlier at a corporate ethics seminar in Barbados, where he asked me, somewhat urgently as I now recall, for the names of a good criminal lawyer, a full-time armed bodyguard, and a reliable plastic surgeon who was willing to operate onboard a sailboat. To this day, Jimbo still shakes his head when he remembers the mistakes he made while packing for his very first trip to prison.

"I packed," Jimbo says, "as if I were going on a business trip!"

It's easy to ridicule Jimbo's comment, and it's fun, too. But in fairness to Jimbo, he had two good excuses for his misconceptions about packing for prison. First, he had never been to prison before; and second, he had suffered a serious head injury months earlier when he was set upon by angry shareholders wielding tree branches and big sticks outside his corporate headquarters.

Jimbo's not alone, however, as many convicted CEOs make the classic "beginner's mistake" of packing for prison as if they were going on a business trip. Not a good business trip, mind you, like your company's annual golf outing in Scottsdale, but a really bad business trip, like that SEC compliance workshop in Trenton that you wisely blew off. The fact that prison is often referred to as "The Gray Bar Hotel" may contribute to this confusion, leading some CEOs to assume that prison will have most of the amenities of a hotel, with the addition of gray bars. I can assure you, however, that the prison yard at Joliet is no Courtyard by Marriott. You will not be enjoying maid service, little mints on the pillows, or in-room movies that do not appear on your bill. And forget about checkout time.

When packing for prison, let me suggest the following step-saver. Make a list of all of the things you would like to bring. Divide that list into three categories: (a) necessities; (b) luxury items; and (c) cigarettes. Now, draw a thick black line through every item on that list except for "cigarettes," and you're through.

That's right. You can forget all about packing your Bose Wave Radio or that terry cloth robe you stole from the Savoy or anything else you think might make your new "home away from home" more comfy. When you arrive at the "Receptions and Departures" area at the prison, the one and only personal item that they are likely to let you bring in with you will be a pack of cigarettes—and that's it.

No one knows exactly why cigarettes came to receive this special exemption, although something tells me that a little thing called the tobacco industry lobby in Washington, D.C., may have played some role. But that's really neither here nor there. If you're a convicted CEO who also happens to be a chain-smoker—and thanks to the pressures of nonstop harassment by the federal government, 98 percent of all convicted CEOs are chain-smokers—the fact that you're allowed to bring cigarettes with you to prison should come as fabulous news. In fact, it's one of the many things that make life behind bars far more enjoyable than life in the corporate world could ever hope to be.

Think I'm exaggerating? Over the past decade, anti-smoking groups have tightened the noose around corporate smokers, virtually banning smoke in the workplace. How many times did you have to excuse yourself from meetings, ride the elevator down thirty floors, and scurry outside for a quick puff—only to have to run back up to the meeting and start the process all over again in another three minutes? By contrast, in most prisons smoking is one of the few activities that is permitted anywhere, any time, by anybody.

Prisoners smoke in their cells, in the dining hall, even while punching each other in the face. At times, it's hard to see your cell mate through the rich, swirling plume of cigarette smoke that fills your cell like a genie freshly released from his bottle. And do the guards complain about secondhand smoke the way those annoying candy-asses in the Human Resources Department of your company used to? Fat chance—because most of the guards are puffing away themselves! For cigarette-loving CEOs used to toiling under the onerous, smoke-free tyranny of the corporate workplace, going to prison will represent the first whiff of freedom they've known in years.

Now, get ready for a major-league curveball. Although cigarettes are the only things prisoners are allowed to bring with them to prison with no questions asked, cigarettes should be the *last* things you consider packing, even if you smoke like a volcano.

Why? It's a simple matter of logic. On the trading floor that every penitentiary eventually becomes, cigarettes are of little or no value, since they are the second-most common commodities in prison, right after concealed weapons. Consequently, bringing cigarettes with you to prison makes about as much sense as bringing cash with you to an ATM. So dump the cigarettes right out and use the empty cigarette pack to smuggle in something that will fetch a much higher sum behind bars: nicotine gum.

I'm letting you in on a little secret: Nicotine gum is the single scarcest and most sought-after contraband in the prison world today. Nearly every prisoner develops a three-pack-a-day habit while he's behind bars, and if he wants to quit—well, then, he's going to have to talk to the fellow with the nicotine gum, won't he? My very first week at Lomax, my small supply of nicotine gum fetched a "street price" of $900—more than enough seed money to get my first start-up business off the ground. Consider nicotine gum your IPO (Invaluable Prison Object) and watch the money roll in.

One final thought: Other than nicotine gum, I'd strongly advise you not to attempt to smuggle in any other items of contraband, especially on your person. There is a very, very good reason for this.

When you first arrive at the prison's "Receptions and Departures" area, you will notice several large, angry-looking prison guards telling you to remove all of your clothing at once. (If they look angry, by the way, don't take it personally: It's probably because they haven't had a cigarette in minutes.) At this point, you will be showered and "deloused." (This latter process afforded the guard who was processing me the chance to comment, somewhat waggishly, that the delousing procedure had been incomplete since I was still standing there. For some prison guards, every night is open-mic night.)

After the delousing is over and done with, you can expect the most thorough search of your body that has ever been performed, culminating in a procedure known as the "booty check." I'd rather not get too graphic here, but let me describe it this way: Remember when you were in talks to acquire another company, and the negotiator from the other side told you to take your offer and put it "where the sun don't shine"? If you had done as you were told, in the course of the booty check the prison guard will find your offer exactly where you put it. And he won't let you keep it, either.

5

Prison Slang:
From Ass-out to Zip Gun

Imagine yourself in a strange new world where the population speaks a barely coherent language that seems designed to confuse, intimidate, and even terrify all newcomers. Every time you ask what something means, your inquiry is greeted with silence, derision, or physical assault. And so you stop asking and start pretending that you understand, nodding in agreement with the nonsense that is spoken around you at a dizzying clip. You may even try your hand at speaking this obscure dialect yourself, even though misusing one word in the wrong situation could result in personal humiliation, ostracism, or worse—far worse.

I'm sure that many of you thought that the place I just described was the typical American prison. Guess again: I was talking about the boardroom of the Ford Motor Company in Detroit, Michigan, based on several eyewitness accounts of what goes on there. But this harrowing description could apply equally well to dozens of other American companies, as well as to some nationally recognized charitable organizations. As anyone who has ever sat through a meaningless PowerPoint presentation or an indecipherable Greenspan speech knows, in the business world, those who can "talk the talk" of business jargon have a tremendous advantage over all others, including over the tiny minority of businessmen who actually know how to form complete English sentences.

The same could be said about prison, with one small distinction: In prison, using the wrong word or expression is less likely to lead to embarrassment and more likely to lead to one's head being shoved down a toilet.

Some convicted CEOs scoff at this comparison, arguing that the jargon of the corporate world is not only easier to understand but is also far less violent and scary than the brutal patois one is likely to discover in a federal penitentiary. As someone who has done a good deal of time in both places, I must respectfully disagree. I ask you: In which environment are you more likely to hear people throw around such frightening terms as "terminate," "liquidate," and "spread"? Where are orders "routed" and "killed," numbers "crunched," and profit estimates "beaten"? Where are takeovers "hostile" and mutual funds "aggressive"?

Yes, I'm afraid that when it comes to creepy jargon, corporations have it all over prisons—it's not even close. If my cell mate Snake were suddenly forced to become the CEO of AOL/Time Warner, he would surely find the language used at the corporate headquarters in New York hair-raising, to say the least. Once he mastered this lingo, though, Snake would probably in some ways be an improvement over that company's current management and might even boost pretax earnings and morale.

One big difference between prisons and corporations, of course, is that many CEOs attend business school for two years before they begin their business careers and thus are able to learn all of the terminology they will ultimately need to use on the job. That is, unless they inherited the CEO position from a family member, in which case they probably enrolled in business school but never actually attended their classes, merely purchasing their term papers over the Internet.

Still, there's no appropriate course of study available to prepare convicted CEOs for the language they will hear in prison; one cannot attend two years of "P-school" to learn the meaning of such useful terms as "foo foo" (deodorant) and "jack mack" (canned fish). The rising tide of CEO convictions is changing all that; reportedly, both Harvard and Wharton are considering adding courses in prison slang to their standard business school curricula. Until they do, however, incarcerated CEOs will be doomed to spend many months in prison having no idea what the hell people are saying to them—a dangerous state of affairs, to say the least.

Every now and then, I'll hear about a prison-bound CEO who doesn't think he needs to make an effort to learn prison slang. He's probably used to having a staff of professionals around him at all times to help explain things he does not understand, such as arcane legal terms, intentionally misleading SEC regulations, and some of the Ten Commandments. Are you one of these stubborn CEOs? If the handcuffs fit, wear them. But I strongly recommend that you shed all such arrogance before you get to the penitentiary. If you were going to spend the next ten to twenty years living in another country, you'd take the time to learn the language spoken there. And prison is definitely another country; specifically, it is a country a lot like North Korea.

In the next few pages, I will attempt to give the newly convicted CEO a crash course in prison slang. One caveat, though: Like any new language, prison slang has so many intricacies, so many subtleties, that you really can't expect to master it without months or perhaps years of practice. Fortunately, many of you will have enough time behind bars to become more fluent than you ever dreamed possible. But in those first few terrifying weeks, staying on top of all of these new words and phrases can be a little too much to ask, especially since you will also be spending much of your time running away from people or hiding behind things.

I recommend you do as I did and get your hands on a Palm Pilot, Visor, or other PDA so that you can download the most commonly used prison slang terms for quick and easy reference. (No need to try to smuggle in a Palm—thanks to the recent influx of convicted CEOs, they're the third most common items in prison, right behind concealed weapons and cigarettes.) Case in point: During my first week at Lomax, in the middle of a prison uprising, a convict named Fist gave me a hard stare and shouted, "Kick rocks, bitch!"—an expression I did not immediately recognize. Fortunately, I was able to consult my Palm and learn, much to my alarm, that he wanted me to leave the area immediately or face the consequences. I didn't need my Palm to translate what those consequences were—the lead pipe he was brandishing spoke a language all its own.

As you download the following glossary of prison terms into your PDA, then, try not to be overwhelmed by the avalanche of new information, and rest assured: If you do your homework, in no time at all you'll be running your neck like a solid peckerwood.

7-Up: Warning that a guard is approaching.

401(k)-Up: Warning that a former shareholder of yours is approaching.

ADX: Administrative Max Florence, considered the highest security prison in the country, where workers must work, eat, and remain locked up in their cells at all times; sometimes also referred to as "Citigroup."

flip the pad: To flip over a mattress in one's prison cell; also, to sell one's Park Avenue co-op to cover legal expenses.

big jab: Lethal injection.

little jab: Reference to your prison sentence in *The Wall Street Journal*'s "Heard on the Street" column.

clavo: Collection or stash; as in, "I hope the IRS doesn't find out about my enormous clavo of Swiss francs in Geneva."

snitch: In prison, a "snitch" is a term for a prisoner who rats out other convicts in order to get special favors; in the corporate world, a "snitch" is sometimes also called a "whistle-blower" and winds up on the cover of *Time* magazine.

ducat: Internal prison pass.

fucat: What a prisoner says after being denied a ducat.

R&D: "Receptions and Departures," the secure location in the prison through which prisoners are admitted and discharged; also refers to what you claimed you were spending your company's funds on when you were actually buying priceless Bugatti motorcars for a stripper.

grunion: Small amount; as in, "Suckers who invested their pension funds in WorldCom now have only a grunion of their money left."

BOP: Abbreviation for Bureau of Prisons; when used as a verb, means to hit over the head with a club, baseball bat, or other heavy object.

make paper: Make parole.

fake paper: Something your company issued way too much of, greatly reducing your chances of ever making paper.

Lay advocate: 1. A so-called "jailhouse lawyer," a prisoner who knows legal rules and procedures and may accompany another prisoner to a hearing; 2. Any member of the legal team of former Enron CEO Kenneth Lay.

four-minute job: Shower; also refers to the tenure of SEC chairman Harvey Pitt.

c-file: The central file, in which critical information on each prisoner is recorded.

c-note: The customary cost of getting the warden to alter the information in one's c-file.

homes: Term of endearment that is an abbreviation for "homeboy"; when combined with the phrase "in the Hamptons," refers to what most convicted CEOs are permitted to keep as part of their plea bargain agreements.

peter-gazer: Convict who stares at other people's private parts while in the shower.

The Peter-Gazer Principle: Widely respected management theory, postulating that all peter-gazers eventually rise beyond their level of competence.

gettin' my [blank] on: Doing something. For example, "gettin' my mack on" means having sex; "gettin' my jack on" means pleasuring oneself; "gettin' my flack on" means hiring a costly publicist to blame your malfeasance on someone else.

copping deuces: To contradict oneself; also known as "testifying before Congress."

donkey dick: Sliced cold cuts; as in, "Whoever invested in Global Crossing must've had donkey dick for brains."

Bush pass: 1. An escape or walk-away; 2. Presidential pardon.

You put me on Front Street, punk: You may have unintentionally divulged sensitive information, much to my detriment.

You got a freak bone a mile long: You excel at thinking "outside the box."

I'mo punch your grille out: I am about to divest you of your teeth.

Prison Food:
Don't Pick Up the Check

My former partner, the internationally renowned fugitive financier Viktor M. Saurian, was a great eater, whether plowing through a nine-course meal while on a fully expensed business trip to the Côte d'Azur, or chewing and swallowing the receipts from that same trip while an FBI agent was pounding on his locked office door. Viktor was a gourmet's gourmet, although I must admit I found his insistence on sitting with his back to the restaurant wall and making me taste his food before he would put it in his mouth a little disconcerting. I'm sure that at this very moment Victor is tucking into a fabulous meal at a four-star eatery in some exotic far-flung tax haven, assuming that Interpol hasn't hunted him down and killed him by now.

In his love of food, Viktor is far from alone, since costly expense account dining has always played a central role in the life of a successful CEO and, for that matter, in the lives of many unsuccessful ones. Even in the middle of a difficult takeover battle or a nail-biting RICO prosecution, a chief executive can always count on a gourmet meal as a consistent source of succor, much as a newborn baby comes to rely upon its mother's teat. In contrast, the prospect of eating institutional food in a drab, depressing prison dining hall that is a breeding ground for both random violence and rabid vermin is not the sort of thing that has most CEOs flipping their Hermès ties over their shoulders in eager anticipation. In fact, a recent poll of newly convicted CEOs reveals that the area in the prison that these former chief executives fear the most is not the shower, as one might expect, but the cafeteria. (The shower, however, did finish a close second.)

Unfortunately for the pampered chief executive, the moment he is incarcerated his dining options dwindle precipitously; in prison, CEO might as well stand for Can't Eat Out. But here's the good news: Adapting to eating in prison after years of living high off the hog— or, should I say, high off the shareholders—is not nearly so tough as most convicted CEOs expect it to be. In fact, if you take a step back for a moment, the similarities between expense account dining and prison dining are both numerous and startling.

In prison, as in the corporate world, you never have to make your own reservations, you never have to pay for your meals, and you never have to wait to be seated—in fact, if you dawdle even for a moment, the guards are likely to hit you. And what about the legendary scenes of prison cafeteria violence so luridly portrayed in Hollywood prison movies? In actuality, these eruptions, while frequent, pale in comparison to the far more violent melee that occurs when a maître d' in New York or Los Angeles fails to recognize a combustible movie executive and gives him an undesirable table near the kitchen or Steven Seagal.

As for the paucity of meal choices on the daily prison menu, this shouldn't take so much getting used to, either. While the convicted CEO probably believes that he had a broad array of choices before him when he sat down to dine at his favorite deluxe eatery, this couldn't be farther from the truth. The dirty little secret about the restaurant world's upper echelon is this: The finer the restaurant, the less influence the diner has over what he eventually finds on his plate. At the most exclusive dining establishments in the world's financial capitals, true power resides with the chef, who usually wields it like a capricious and infantile tyrant. Don't try to order steak frites or crab cakes at one of these places—you'll have what the resident culinary genius wants you to have, whether you can stomach it or not. Odd, isn't it, that most CEOs have no problem with this sort of dietary torture when they are sitting in the banquette of a so-called "hot" restaurant, yet cry foul at the same practice when they encounter it in a prison cafeteria? If CEOs could be convicted for hypocrisy, in addition to fraud and embezzlement, every executive suite in the country would be suddenly vacant.

Given that the chasm between expense account dining and prison dining is not nearly so great as you thought, here's a little tip for making the most of your time in the prison cafeteria. Try to imagine that you are in an exclusive gourmet restaurant, sitting within air-kissing distance of Daniel Day Lewis and Sting. If you close your eyes and imagine that the food put before you in the prison cafeteria is the latest offering of a temperamental chef's "Spring Tasting Menu" or "Autumn Harvest Delectation Sampler" rather than a plateful of rancid slop you had no hand in choosing, mealtime behind bars will become far more enjoyable right from the get-go. There's a larger lesson in this, and a valuable one at that: Generally speaking, most aspects of prison life will become much more pleasurable, or at least endurable, if you try to imagine that something other than what is actually going on is going on. This skill of compartmentalizing two entirely different realities in your brain shouldn't be hard for you to master—it's just like keeping two different sets of books.

One final point about food: While it is true that dining options are seriously limited in the prison cafeteria, choices do exist. All you have to do is pretend to be religious. At Lomax, for example, I noticed that so-called "special meals" for members of certain religious faiths were usually offered and were often far more appetizing than what the rest of the prison population was being served. Therefore, I recommend that all convicted

CEOs memorize a few simple prayers from each of the major religions of the world before they are even incarcerated, since authentic-sounding religious chanting or singing can often fool the cafeteria workers into serving them the much tastier fare that's available.

Now that we've solved the problem of eating in prison, which turned out to be not such a big problem after all, what about drinking?

Many CEOs, of course, love wine even more than they love food, and the prospect of spending five, ten, or more years without access to their favorite Bordeaux or Montrachet is, as far as they're concerned, cruel and unusual punishment. The absence of wine behind bars, however, is largely a myth. While it may be true that an imprisoned CEO is unlikely to find a bottle that won raves in the latest issue of *Wine Spectator,* or even *Wino Spectator,* if he's open-minded enough, he'll soon come to enjoy the next best thing: a wine-like beverage indigenous to prisons called "pruno." Also called "chalk" or "raisin jack," pruno is made by enterprising prisoners themselves, using fruit, yeast, sugar, and other ingredients stolen from the prison cafeteria, then carefully fermented in black plastic bags or in the prisoner's own toilet bowl. If all of this sounds unappetizing, remember: At least the French didn't stick their feet in it.

Before you turn up your nose at pruno—which I've rather grown to like, especially with a nice cheese—hear me out. Over the years, it's been my observation that what most CEOs really love about wine isn't so much drinking it, but rather showing off their knowledge about it in order to make the people they're dining with feel crummy. In this regard, pruno gets it done like no other wine on the planet. Once your prison sentence is complete and you're back on the outside, you'll have years of one-upmanship to look forward to as you brag to your wine-expert pals about all the great prunos you enjoyed behind bars: A Folsom '97, perhaps, or a San Quentin '99. Just make sure that if they ask how pruno is spelled, you say "pruneaux," so that they'll be convinced it's some rare French varietal they've inexplicably missed out on. If you're lucky, they'll spend the next thirty years trying to hunt it down while on wine-tasting tours of the Loire Valley, perhaps ruining their lives in the process.

When you think about it, navigating the mysterious worlds of food and wine behind bars is no different from figuring out where to eat in a strange new city you're visiting for the first time. I'm sure you can recall the many times you landed in a foreign capital to sell some local bankers on a tax-dodging currency-trading scheme of yours—even if, at your trial, you said you couldn't recall doing any of this. How did you decide where to eat in those places you'd never been before? Simple: Your assistant probably flipped through a Zagat guide and chose the most overpriced restaurant in town, and you were off to the races.

Unfortunately, even though Zagat's most loyal readers—executives with grotesquely bloated expense accounts—are now headed for the pokey, Zagat has not yet stepped up to the plate and issued a dining guide to our nation's penitentiaries. In an attempt to fill this regrettable void, I decided to create such a guide myself, using survey questionnaires filled out by thousands of experts in the world of fine prison dining—convicted CEOs like me. Here, then, is my very own Zagat guide to the top five prisons in America, rated by food, decor, service, and overall dining experience:

U.S. Penitentiary Marion (Marion, Illinois)

Surveyors rave about this "low-security facility with high-quality cuisine," which, despite recent challenges from innovative prison chefs elsewhere in the federal system, remains the gold standard for prison food everywhere. While some inmates say that the food "doesn't live up to the hype," most surveyors agree that the main courses "taste better than they look" and "rarely make you ill"; still, Marion's detractors say the food's "not worth getting stabbed on line for."

U.S. Penitentiary Leavenworth (Leavenworth, Kansas)

"You won't want to be paroled" after tasting the sumptuous meals at this old heartland favorite, which recently changed chefs when its former cook was sidelined in a mysterious scalding accident. With desserts that "you can usually keep down" and a "first-rate" selection of pruno, it's no wonder that surveyors rate Leavenworth the one prison "you'd want to break into, not out of."

Federal Correctional Institution Butner (Butner, North Carolina)

If you can "get past the name," you'll want to "strap on the feedbag" at legend-in-the-making Butner, where the food is generally "edible," if not always "identifiable." Inmates say "you won't want to miss these meals" even if your "teeth" have been "knocked out," making it "difficult" to "eat." Some surveyors complained about poultry dishes that "even the Birdman of Alcatraz wouldn't recognize as chicken," while others said the kitchen suffered from a combination of "disinterest and dysentery"; still, most inmates agree that if you are locked up at Butner, this is "the only place to eat."

U.S. Penitentiary Lompoc (Lompoc, California)
Johnny Cash "wouldn't have been singing the blues" if he'd been stuck in Lompoc, say surveyors who call the meals here "rarely lethal." Despite the generally passable food ratings, some surveyors complain that the service ranges from "leisurely" to "downright hostile," and warn inmates not to linger too long over their slop, since there are "extremely rude" prison guards standing by to "kick" your "ass."

U.S. Penitentiary Terre Haute (Terre Haute, Indiana)
Home to a number of inmates on federal death row, the storied kitchen at Terre Haute has more than its share of "tough customers" who, when it comes to their last meals, can be as "finicky as Morris the Cat." Still, the USP Terre Haute chef manages to produce "amazing" made-to-order meals for this notoriously "hard-to-please" group, with such special requests as "tender" Porterhouse steak, "exquisite" French fries, and chocolate pudding that is literally "to die for"; in the words of one satisfied surveyor, "you'll wish your last meal wasn't."

7

The Seven Habits of Highly Effective Prisoners™

Back in the good old days, when the bull market seemed unstoppable and I seemed unindictable, Shamco's pharmaceutical arm was the jewel in our jerry-built corporate crown. But even that storied division could cough up a real lulu every now and then. I remember when we attempted to steal market share away from the blockbuster drug Viagra by launching a competing medication of our own called HorniMax. In a shrewd marketing move to trump Viagra's claims of treating ED (Erectile Dysfunction), we purported that HorniMax could successfully eradicate PADD (Penile Attention Deficit Disorder). HorniMax smelled like a hit to us, and once we announced that we had twenty million little yellow pills ready to be shipped and an offer out to one of the Backstreet Boys to be its commercial pitchman, the stock market seemed to agree.

Then disaster struck. The drug, which had breezed through the FDA approval process, turned out not to treat PADD at all but instead made those men who took it develop severe hay fever–like symptoms when sexually aroused. After a series of consumer complaints and some fairly brutal congressional hearings, one of the FDA officials who had been part of the approval decision broke down and confessed that he had accepted a time share in Maui and a vintage Alfa Romeo in exchange for his thumbs-up. The aftermath wasn't pretty for Shamco. Several of the executives involved in the HorniMax scandal are currently serving time in prisons across the country—yet another example of the federal government pouncing on a convenient scapegoat while the real culprit, male impotence, goes unpunished.

Why do I mention this less than happy tale from the Shamco corporate crypt? Because it speaks to a principle that's critical to your success in prison: the principle of trial and error. We may have struck out with Horni-Max, but the next time we stepped up to the plate with a new male performance drug, Bonutrin, we hit a home run. What did we do differently? We paid off the necessary FDA officials in untraceable hundred-dollar bills and told them in no uncertain terms that if they sang to the feds we'd make them regret it, big-time. Learning from our mistakes certainly paid off: Even though Bonutrin was no more effective than HorniMax, it was the most-written prescription in America that year.

Trial and error have been my constant companions in prison—particularly error. I'll never forget, on the day of my arrival here, when I forgot to turn off the "Flight of the Bumblebee" ringer on my cell phone, inspiring Snake to push my head between two of our cell's steel bars in retaliation. Did I sit there crying, feeling sorry for myself? Yes, for hours on end, but I also thought to myself, "Lesson learned."

Every time I learned a new lesson from one of my mistakes at Lomax, I wrote it down, and eventually, certain patterns—paradigms, if you will—began to emerge. I realized that all behavior in prison could be broken down into these paradigms, and that every prisoner could improve his performance through a series of "paradigm shifts," although in the case of some prisoners, only antipsychotic medication really seems to do the trick. I distilled this knowledge into a series of helpful practices, or "habits," that I am ready to share with you now: habits I call the Seven Habits of Highly Effective Prisoners™.

What are the Seven Habits? Simply put, they are the keys to gaining the upper hand in the tooth-and-claw, dog-eat-dog, prisoner-kick-prisoner-in-the-head struggle taking place each and every day in America's penitentiaries. Ignore these habits at your peril; follow them, and you'll go from "bitch" to "boss" in a matter of weeks.

You may be wondering, why just seven habits? Why

not eight, for example, or nine? Why not really shoot my wad and go for one hundred habits? Good questions all. If you'll shut your pie-hole for a minute I'll try to answer them.

You may be interested in knowing that, before I narrowed down my list to the final seven, I first eliminated close to nine hundred *bad* habits I observed while behind bars—habits I call the Almost Nine Hundred Bad Habits of Highly Ineffective Prisoners™. Some CEOs have asked that I publish a complete list of these bad habits, so that they'll know what practices to avoid while behind bars. As helpful as that would be, space limitations unfortunately prevent me from doing so— and if you're in prison right now, I really don't have to explain the concept of space limitations to you. But just to give you a general flavor, the top three most common Bad Habits of Highly Ineffective Prisoners would be these: (1) making fun of other prisoners' faces or physiques; (2) "ratting out" or "dropping a dime on" another inmate while the inmate you are snitching on can clearly see and hear you doing it; and (3) attempting to tunnel your way out of the prison with a plastic spoon.

Some CEOs will want to learn more good habits than the seven I enumerate. Still other CEOs will consider seven habits more than enough and will chafe at the notion of having to read all seven. Their impatience, while babyish, doesn't surprise me. CEOs may be known for their love of eating but they are hardly known for their love of reading. Anyone who's seen the large type and prairie-like margins in the average business best-seller can readily attest to this fact. Sure, CEOs will pretend to be interested in the "important" and talked-about books of the moment, just as I lied and told people that I was reading that really long book about John Adams a couple of summers ago. But the truth is, most chief executives would rather do anything than read, even run on a treadmill or spend time with their families. Their meager appetite for reading is unlikely to increase markedly in prison, where there is so much else competing for their attention, such as other convicts' bodies hurtling through the air at them without warning.

I've recently learned that another author, attempting to cash in on the short attention span of the average incarcerated CEO, is about to publish a thirty-eight-page survival guide to prison entitled the *One-Minute Prisoner*™. If you honestly think you will be well served by the superficial effort of some amoral hack who's out to make a quick buck at the expense of an unsuspecting public, by all means, have a loved one smuggle that little book into prison for you inside your very next banana loaf. But to the more discerning among you, I would offer these words of caution: Accept no substitutes. Only by taking the time to learn all Seven Habits of Highly Effective Prisoners™ can the former CEO hope to make his time behind bars the highly profitable experience it can be. So set aside the eight or nine minutes necessary to read this chapter, and let's begin.

Habit #1: Be Proactive

CEOs are used to taking the reins at their companies and leading through the force of their own personalities, however obnoxious and repellent those personalities may be. It is odd, then, that these same CEOs become the very epitome of submissiveness once they set foot in prison. The radical change in environment and stimuli may have something to do with this uncharacteristic shift from "proactive" to "reactive" behavior. All of a sudden, the former CEO is being called "punk" or "bitch" or "old lady" rather than "boss" or "sir" or "Mr. Taubman." These new, less flattering epithets do little to make a CEO feel that he is in charge of what is happening around him—or to him. "If someone calls you 'bitch' often enough, pretty soon you start saying to yourself, 'Hey, maybe I *am* a bitch,' " one CEO told me recently. I couldn't put it better myself.

A good way for a convicted CEO to determine if he has already started down this slippery slope to reactive behavior is by listening to the way he talks. Our language provides us with diagnostic clues as to whether we are being proactive or reactive, as the following examples clearly show:

Reactive Language	Proactive Language
1. Please don't hit me with that big thing.	1. I'mo bust a grape, peckerwood.
2. Could you please put that down?	2. I'mo peal your cap, monkey mouth.
3. Oof!	3. (to guard) I didn't do nothin'.

If you've found yourself saying any of the expressions in the column on the left, and none of the ones on the right, then you've come to this chapter not a moment too soon, for you may already be well on your way to becoming a punk-ass bitch.

In prison, every CEO faces a simple choice: "Act or be acted upon." The following story, shared with me by a CEO currently doing time in Colorado for using accounting practices that are only recognized in certain provinces of Kazakhstan, illustrates this point:

Alan G. (not his real last initial) found himself slipping into reactive behavior the moment he began his prison sentence. Specifically, he was terrified of becoming caught in a prison riot and suffering serious bodily injury—far from an irrational phobia, given his fellow inmates' yen for rioting and hurting one another. The only problem with having such a fear, as Alan G. soon discovered, was that once other prisoners find out you are fearful, they tend to single you out for the most vicious attacks, such as banging your head repeatedly against a sink or a big rock. If ever a CEO's attitude was crying out for a "paradigm shift," it was Alan G.'s.

Alan G. decided to make the shift from being reactive to being proactive, in the simplest, most logical way he knew how: by starting prison riots himself, on an almost daily basis. Knowing when and how prison riots would occur and causing them to start on a schedule of his own choosing went a long way toward making Alan G. feel empowered. What's more, other prisoners started looking upon him as a dangerously insane or "psycho" inmate who might "nut out" without warning. Consequently, they now tend to stay far out of his way and look upon him fearfully—beginning *their* gradual transformation into punk-ass bitches. This paradigm shift business, it turns out, works in both directions.

The only downside of Alan G.'s shift from reactive to proactive behavior is that he is now put in solitary at least once a week—but here, at least, is one Highly Effective Prisoner who doesn't see that as a downside. "I do some of my best thinking in solitary," Alan G. says. I couldn't agree more, which is why Habit #1 is the #1 Habit.

Habit #2: Begin With the End in Mind
Another key to becoming a Highly Effective Prisoner is to visualize, if you can, how you would like to be remembered as a prisoner on the day when you are eventually released. An even more important key is to visualize your release occurring much, much sooner than anyone, including the judge who sentenced you, ever imagined it happening.

Of course, if you have followed Habit #1 ("Be Proactive"), you've got a bit of a dilemma on your hands. If you are initiating a prison riot every day and being sent to solitary, you are not only hurting the way you will be remembered on the day of your release, but you are also pushing your release date much farther into the future than you'd probably enjoy visualizing. While good behavior often results in reduced sentences, bad behavior, such as starting daily riots, results in just the opposite. If you're not careful, you could be looking at a scenario in which the President who pardons you is named either Barb or Jenna Bush.

Does Habit #1, then, make Habit #2 impossible, or at the very least, really hard? Not at all. In order to counteract the negative effects of starting so many riots, a CEO can do much to get back in the good graces of the warden. For starters, he can get in the habit of informing on other inmates, whether they are guilty of any infractions or not. For those CEOs who are used to blaming their own malfeasance on their Big Five accounting firm, snitching on fellow convicts should hardly be a new skill set. Of all of the seven habits, this one is my favorite, hands-down.

Some of you may question this advice, since I earlier singled out snitching as one of the top three bad habits to avoid while behind bars. That's correct—but I took great pains to specify that I meant snitching when the person you're snitching on *can see or hear you do it*. As you will see, there is a fine line between a bad habit and a good habit; generally speaking, a bad habit becomes a good habit if you don't get caught doing it.

Habit #3: Put First Things First

Like many CEOs, Robert F. dreaded setting foot in the prison shower. Fearful of being punished for "peter-gazing" if his gaze happened to fall on another inmate's private parts, he would close his eyes the moment he stepped into the shower room. Unfortunately, this measure backfired catastrophically. Unable to see anything, Robert F. repeatedly bumped into naked prisoners or mistakenly reached for what he thought was a shower knob but was actually something else. Both of these faux pas resulted in far more serious repercussions than what he would have suffered had he just kept his eyes open to begin with.

Clearly, Robert F. needed to make a "paradigm shift" and "put first things first": establish a priority and act upon it accordingly. He realized that his true priority was not avoiding "peter-gazing" per se, but was, in fact, getting out of the shower and back into his clothes as quickly as possible. Robert F. realized that once he was fully clothed he could then apply himself to his other important priorities—namely, starting prison riots and snitching on fellow inmates.

Today when Robert F. takes a shower, he enters the shower room with his head held high, his eyes wide open, and—most important—his body fully clothed, enabling him to complete his shower in well under twelve seconds. Not only does his clothing provide him with some measure of protection, but wearing it into the shower reinforces the impression that he is crazy or psycho and could nut out without warning—which, as we have discussed, is never a bad reputation for a prisoner to have.

Habit #4: Think "Win/Win"

The so-called "Win/Win" strategy is surprisingly rare behind bars, greatly outnumbered by the "Win/Scream with Pain" strategy, the "Win/Crumple to the Floor" strategy, and even the much-dreaded "Win/Die" strategy. It's a shame.

I realized early on in my stay at Lomax that I would have to think "Win/Win" if I was ever going to get my cell mate Snake on the same page with me, or at least get him to stop swinging his tire iron at my head. Getting Snake to be a team player presented a serious challenge, however. How could I give a hardened career criminal who had nothing to lose and who could asphyxiate me with one hand tied behind his back an incentive to root for my success?

Easy: I made him a shareholder.

On my third day behind bars, flush with cash from my

recent sales of nicotine gum, I flashed a roll of twenties at Snake and told him there was plenty more where that came from. (Hardened career criminals and FDA officials, at the end of the day, have more in common than either would probably care to admit.) I let Snake know that I intended to start up a major corporation at Lomax and issued 10,000 Class B (nonvoting) shares to him right then and there in our cell. I also told him that if he held on to these shares, they would gradually appreciate in value, outperforming bonds, cash, and real estate, and would someday finance his retirement. By thinking "Win/Win," I not only won Snake over to my side but I secured his services as a bodyguard—because by protecting me, Snake was protecting the value of his nest egg.

One caveat: While the allure of being a shareholder proved powerful for Snake, it may not be equally persuasive for all prisoners. As a general rule of thumb, this particular "Win/Win" strategy works best on prisoners who have not opened a newspaper or seen the news on television for the last two to three years.

Habit #5: Seek First to Understand, Then to Be Understood

This habit is actually a lot of fun. Remember all of that tricky prison slang you learned way back in Chapter 5? If you've done your homework right, by now you will have committed all of those colorful words to memory, in addition to the thousand or so synonyms that prisoners have for "homemade knife." You've finished the first part of this habit—the "seek first to understand" part. Now it's payback time!

The most potent weapon behind bars, actually, is not a homemade knife—it is the language that prisoners use to intimidate, bully, and keep one another perpetually off-balance. When you first arrived in prison, your job was to understand your fellow convicts. Now that you are gaining in confidence and mojo, it is time for *them* to understand *you*. If you make this task difficult enough for them, you will swiftly gain dominance over them. Over time, that means you will be able to force them to do your bidding, even to commit acts that may be against the law. In other words, you will become their CEO.

In order to make their job of understanding you as tough as possible, it is important that you start speaking in an exotic tongue almost no one on the planet could ever hope to comprehend. To this end, I recommend creating an altogether new language from the transcripts of the congressional hearings on the Enron bankruptcy. Sprinkle into your conversation such terms as GAAP (Generally Accepted Accounting Principles), GAAS (Generally Accepted Auditing Standards), and SPEs (Special Purpose Entities), and watch your fellow inmates crumble under an avalanche of perplexity.

As I said before, this habit is a lot of fun.

Habit #6: Synergize

While I have drawn many comparisons between the worlds of prison and business in this book, when it comes to the concept of synergy those two worlds could not be more dissimilar.

"Synergy" is a much-used buzzword in the business world, especially in so-called "vertically integrated" media corporations. At the French media giant Vivendi, for example, the word "synergy" is used every 1.5 seconds, despite the fact that the executives there have no idea what it means—even the ones who speak English. While executives at media corporations may love to talk about synergy, particularly at super-investor Herb Allen's annual Sun Valley powwow, there is absolutely no evidence that synergy has ever existed in any of these companies, even in trace amounts.

In prison, on the other hand, synergy is very much alive and well. If you've been practicing the five habits as I've described them, you've probably already noticed just how well these habits are working together in a synergistic way:

When you first arrived at prison, you were reactive, intimidated by your cell mate, confused about the language prisoners were using, and afraid of stepping into the shower.

Now, thanks to the habits, you're proactive, starting riots every day, and making the other inmates believe that you are always about to nut out and therefore are nobody to mess with. Thanks to your use of incomprehensible Enron-speak, your fellow convicts now strain to understand you—but they pretend to nonetheless, for two reasons. First, because they work for you, and people always pretend to understand their boss; and second, because they are your shareholders, and shareholders always want to believe that the CEO of the company they hold shares in is making sense, even when he is spewing utter gibberish. Their livelihood depends on you now, so they'll be the last people on Earth to say that "the emperor has no clothes"—especially now that you, the emperor, take your showers with all of your clothes on.

Sweet.

Habit #7: Sharpen the Saw

Incarcerated executives, preoccupied with practicing the first six habits, often forget about this seventh habit, which may be the most important one of all. In short, they forget to take the time to "Sharpen the Saw."

When I say, "Sharpen the Saw," what exactly do I mean? Do I mean, take the time to renew yourself, mentally and physically? Or am I driving at something far deeper—that you should take the time to renew yourself spiritually, socially, and emotionally?

Actually, when I say you must "Sharpen the Saw," I don't mean any of those things. I mean that you should get your hands on a saw and sharpen it. In prison, it's really useful to have a sharp saw.

8

Prison Cell Feng Shui

If you have practiced the seven habits as detailed in the previous chapter, by now you should be solidly installed as the CEO of the prison population and lord of all you survey. You've probably noticed, based on the wary looks your fellow prisoners are giving you, that you're more feared than loved. That's okay. In fact, in prison it's a good thing to be feared, while being loved is just about the last thing you want to be.

Now you're ready to get to work starting up your business, and for that you will need an office befitting your hard-earned title of CEO. Your choice of office space, of course, was much greater when you were running a Fortune 500 corporation. In those days, commercial real estate companies practically threw themselves at you in the knowledge that you spent your company's money like a drunken sailor. In prison, on the other hand, your office is likely to be a nine-by-nine–foot prison cell with iron bars and no window—far from a status symbol, but more than adequate for your needs. The key to making your workplace contribute to your goals is achieving harmony with it—and there is no better way to achieve that harmony than through the art of feng shui.

Feng shui (pronounced "fung-schway") is a term one rarely hears in prison, in part because mispronouncing it can create such havoc. But this ancient Chinese art of creating the perfect environment will help your prison office make up in tranquility, harmony, and good vibes what it lacks in ventilation, heat, and functioning plumbing.

The average prisoner finds his cell overly spartan, a common complaint being that "there isn't any stuff in it." Ironically, the very emptiness of a prison cell, according to the principles of feng shui, is a source of great spiritual power. Creating a clutter-free environment, feng shui teaches us, is the first prerequisite to increasing *chi* (pronounced "chee") or energy—not to be confused with the prison term "cheese eater," meaning informant. In fact, many executives in the corporate world spend thousands of dollars hiring feng shui consultants to reduce the clutter in their offices. Invariably, these experts advise them to discard unnecessary and distracting objects, like bulky books filled with accounting standards and IRS regulations. Such costly advisers will be entirely unnecessary for you now that you're in prison. Thanks to the near-total absence of anything in your cell to begin with, you are already halfway on the road to achieving a clutter-free atmosphere and maximum *chi*.

Beyond maintaining his cell's near-total emptiness, there is much that an incarcerated CEO can do to make sure that his workplace hews sufficiently to the principles of feng shui. Here, then, is a brief checklist of the steps you should take to create optimum harmony with your prison cell:

- **Arrange your bunk so that you face the bars, not away from them.** Facing the wall of your cell has a negative impact on *chi,* while looking out through the bars creates a wide-open feeling, increasing *chi.* In addition to all of these *chi* benefits, facing outward helps you to see if a guard is coming, which can be helpful if you are in the middle of a transaction involving big stacks of money and weapons.

- **Harness the positive forces that flow through your prison cell.** Feng shui teaches us that different directions govern different positive forces within our environment. "North," for example, governs career and business success, while "South" governs fame and "Southwest" governs your relationships. One of the upsides of living in a nine-by-nine cell is that you can stand in the middle of it, wave your arms around, and soak up all of these positive forces at the same time.

- **Be comfortable with your office equipment.** It is important to have office equipment in your cell that you feel comfortable with and whose operation you fully understand. To shred documents, for example, choose the most efficient and reliable piece of equipment available to you: your newly submissive cell mate. Snake, for example, can chew and swallow up to ten document pages per minute. Talk about *chi*!

- **Improve the lighting in your cell.** The lighting in most prison cells is inadequate for the amount of reading you will have to do, especially as your business begins to generate the mountains of intentionally confusing paperwork and misleading financial statements that are the mother's milk of American capitalism. While most prisons refuse to provide you with a proper desk lamp, this is no great loss, since you will not have a desk, either. Your best bet to achieve better lighting is this: Bribe a guard to sneak you into the warden's office whenever he's not there so that you can use his desk, lamp, and coffee machine, for that matter. Feng shui, at the end of the day, only takes you so far.

Bringing Six Sigma to Sing Sing

How does one start up a great business behind bars—
a business that will be, much like the prison in which it
was hatched, "built to last"?

Every great prison business, in my experience, starts
with a great idea. In my case, I stumbled on just such an
idea almost by accident.

One day, while breaking rocks in the prison yard, I
noticed two prisoners a short distance away from me
swinging away at each other with sledgehammers. The

two convicts inflicted major damage on each other until the guards, who had been off on a cigarette break, finally separated them. While both inmates appeared to be seriously injured, and only one of them seemed to be alive, I noticed that their jumpsuits were remarkably unscathed. I thought to myself, "Who besides prisoners could use an outfit that stands up to so much punishment?" A split-second later, the inspiration came to me.

Soccer moms.

The lifestyle of your average soccer mom, it occurred to me, is every bit as violent as that of the average prisoner in a federal penitentiary—maybe even more so. Case in point: The typical post-soccer game free-for-all, in which the moms have at each other with fists, nails, teeth, and handbags, is easily ten times more destructive than a garden-variety prison riot. Having said that, the women involved in these donnybrooks are clearly not dressed appropriately for battle, wearing Ralph Lauren, Prada, and DKNY instead of a uniform that would hold up under all of the hitting, scratching, and biting that's involved. I think you see where I'm going with this.

Fast-forward.

If you look around any suburban shopping mall these days, you're bound to see the suburban women wearing one item that has become more or less the standard uniform of pissed-off soccer moms everywhere: an orange "prison-type" jumpsuit, stenciled with the words, PROPERTY OF U.S. PENITENTIARY LOMAX.

When they plunked down their $899 to buy this super-chic item, these soccer moms probably assumed it was the creation of some New York designer giving his witty "take" on prison uniforms and making a cutting-edge fashion statement in the process. Little did they suspect that the outfits they are now wearing to PTA meetings and Pilates classes are actually real prison uniforms that are, in fact, property of the United States Penitentiary Lomax—requisitioned at a cost of $24 a suit.

What's more, they'd have no way of guessing that these same jumpsuits were shipped out of the prison to suburban retail outlets by a company founded and run by yours truly—a company I dubbed "Scamco." By operating this business without the knowledge of the warden, the assistant warden, or any of the nine associate wardens, in the last quarter alone Scamco rang up North American prison jumpsuit sales in the amount of $350 million. Given our incredibly low overhead, much of that $350 million is pure profit, contributing to a balance sheet that I didn't even have to fudge to make look good—a first for me.

Impressed? You should be, but I certainly don't deserve all of the credit. A lot of it should go to the convicts I had working for me, the greatest captive workforce I've ever seen. But they and I could never have made the company a success if I had not first implemented the organizational quality system made legendary by "Neutron Jack" Welch of GE: the system known as Six Sigma.

I selected Six Sigma as the quality management system for my new business after rejecting the best-known alternative, the once heralded system known as Total Quality Management (TQM). Where does Six Sigma succeed where Total Quality Management fails? After reading books on both systems, I found that I could understand only 18 percent of the Total Quality Management system, while I understood a full 29 percent of Six Sigma. Given those numbers, it was no contest.

When I decided to start up a billion-dollar fashion empire from within the walls of a high-security prison, Challenge One was this: How could I keep a population of over four thousand hardened criminals—many of whom had tried to kill each other at one point or another during the previous week—working as a team to achieve the same goals? Enter Six Sigma.

First, I chose nine convicts to be so-called Six Sigma "Black Belts," highly skilled Six Sigma "coaches" who would train, motivate, and, in a general way, scare the shit out of all their subordinates. In choosing your Six Sigma "Black Belts," it is highly advisable that you choose nine convicts who, in addition to being "Black Belts" in Six Sigma, are also "Black Belts" in karate. Six Sigma works best, I've found, when the top managers have hands that are lethal weapons, capable of snapping subordinates' necks or spines like matchsticks if the goals dictated by Six Sigma are not met. These "Black Belts" send a clear signal: It's the Six Sigma Way or the highway!

Once chosen, the "Black Belts" had special coaching sessions with their Six Sigma teams every day in the prison shower. With the nozzles turned up full blast to prevent any members of the prison staff from listening in on these all-important coaching sessions, the "Black Belts" shouted key Six Sigma questions at their naked, lathered-up team members:

1. How many prison jumpsuits have your friends/loved ones smuggled out of the prison this week?

2. How many jumpsuits have you told the guards in your block were "stolen" from your body when you slept at night this week, or mysteriously "disintegrated" without warning?

3. How many retail outlets have you personally contacted on your cell phone to determine their level of satisfaction with the shipment of jumpsuits they received this week, as well as to obtain additional orders for more and more jumpsuits?

4. How many guards or other prison workers have you bribed this week with nicotine gum, cash, or Class B shares to keep them quiet about all of these jumpsuits we've been selling?

5. How many times have I told you not to "peter-gaze" while you're in the shower? Cut it out or I'll kick your ass.

The last question on that list was the contribution of Snake, who quickly became one of my most effective "Black Belts" because of his unique ability to discern what motivates prisoners and what does not.

In addition to controlling quality, Six Sigma has been the key to keeping our supply chain/distribution system at Lomax working like a well-oiled machine. Here's an example. When the warden started noticing that hundreds of prison jumpsuits were missing each week, he took immediate action: He began ordering hundreds of new jumpsuits from a government-run supply company. Had there been any time lag in our receiving these new jumpsuits, processing them, and shipping them out again to our retail outlets across the country, our profit margins as well as our customer satisfaction levels would have been adversely impacted. However, by posting Six Sigma team members at every key point along the supply chain—from the guards at the gate, to the workers at the loading dock, to the administrative assistants in the warden's office—the new jumpsuits were often shipped out on the same day they arrived at the prison, without ever touching a prisoner's back. Some people might call that a miracle. In a sense, I suppose, it is: the miracle of Six Sigma.

Will Six Sigma work in every prison-based enterprise? It's too early to tell, but so far, the results are encouraging. A CEO friend of mine who's doing time in California is running a prosperous business manufacturing vanity license plates that the DMV doesn't have the slightest inkling of, and he said his profits are up an astounding 9,000 percent thanks to efficiencies made possible by Six Sigma. "Using Six Sigma, I can stay on top of what every prisoner is doing every hour of the day," this happy CEO writes. "All I can say is, it's a good thing the Federal Bureau of Prisons doesn't believe in it."

10

Female CEOs:
Breaking Through the Concrete Ceiling

Although the government prosecutors accused me of many things, including using monies from Shamco's workmen's compensation account to build a 12,000-square-foot humidor, the one thing they never accused me of was sexism. But such an accusation could be leveled against me with some justification if I did not devote at least one chapter to the unique challenges facing female CEOs who find themselves behind bars. And since sexism is pretty much the only thing I have not yet been found guilty of, I'd like to keep it that way.

I probably should mention at this juncture that even though I was never personally accused of sexism, Shamco has taken a few cheap shots on that score. Our reputation was unfairly tarnished shortly after we went into Chapter Eleven, when several of Shamco's former female staff members elected to pose for a much-ballyhooed "Women of Shamco" pictorial in a so-called "laddie" magazine called *Rack*. The feature, in which the women were shown feeding their clothing into high-speed paper shredders, may have led some readers to suppose that we at Shamco were preoccupied with sex when, in reality, most of the time we were just obsessed with staying one step ahead of the FBI.

But Shamco had to confront charges of sexism long before that sleazy pictorial even appeared. Back in the days when Shamco was still a going concern and its executives were still free to roam the streets, a so-called company "whistle-blower" took it upon herself to charge the company with a variety of misdeeds, including what she called "creating a hostile work environment." All I can say to that is, well, duh—people are going to be hostile to you if you go around blowing your whistle on them all the livelong day. Frankly, I don't need a whistle-blower to tell me what's wrong with my company, since I tend to be my own harshest critic. But when I think back on what a female-friendly company Shamco was, I really don't have the slightest idea what that whistle-blower was tooting about.

Unlike some notorious Wall Street firms whose names I won't mention, at Shamco we never had a so-called "Boom-Boom Room" in which female staff members were subjected to the leering harassment of their male coworkers. In fact, the only wet T-shirt contest ever held in the history of Shamco took place at the nearby Señor Wiggles Grill and Bar and starred male executives strutting their stuff for the benefit of female staff members. The event was my idea, a direct response to our whistle-blower's charges; I thought it was a chance to show that we actually catered to women by creating an evening of entertainment that they especially would enjoy. Even though no female staff members actually showed up that night at Señor Wiggles, I still think the event had enormous symbolic value since it sent the message that, at Shamco, equality ruled.

That was certainly true in the executive suite. At our company, women filled many of the highest executive positions and were entrusted with the most important tasks, including breaking into locked offices to delete e-mails and perjuring themselves in federal court. As a result, to this day Shamco has the largest number of female executives behind bars of any former Fortune 500 company. Although I'm extremely proud of this statistic, once again I'm not asking for credit—the credit, I believe, rightfully belongs to these hardworking women themselves.

Given how many of Shamco's female executives are currently serving lengthy prison sentences, I was very disappointed that none of them agreed to talk with me about their experiences behind bars for the purposes of this chapter. Furthermore, I thought that many of the angry, expletive-laden letters they sent in reply to my written queries were entirely uncalled for and hurtful.

However, I chalk up some of their bitterness to the struggles they are currently enduring in prison, a work environment ten times more "hostile" than Shamco ever was, no matter what Little Miss Whistle-blower has to say about it.

Fortunately, perhaps the most celebrated female executive behind bars today was willing to share her prison experiences with me: Clarissa Hoyden, former CEO of Clarissa Hoyden Megalomedia, a woman whose relentless attention to the details of homemaking, gardening, and entertaining inspired tabloid wags to dub her "The Domestic Despot."

Starting with her very first business plan, which she drew up on her kitchen table with a tube of cake-decorating gel, Clarissa Hoyden created a multibillion-dollar consumer products/media empire from what some clinical psychologists would call an untreated mood disorder. Starting by publishing such helpful books as *Clarissa Hoyden Cooking* and *Clarissa Hoyden Party Giving* and *Clarissa Hoyden Getting Your Guests to Leave Before They Eat You Out of House and Home,* Clarissa gradually moved into the lucrative world of television programs and instructional videos, and ultimately became a leading supplier of affordable but high-quality household linens, tableware, and short- to medium-range ballistic missile systems. Defying her critics, Clarissa kept her eye on the prize and achieved the American dream: By the age of forty-one, she was widely considered the most hated woman in the United States.

But then, in August 2002, Clarissa's dream came crashing to earth. She had spent an idyllic day sailing off the coast of Montauk, Long Island, onboard her seventy-foot power cruiser, The S.S. *Control Freak*. From the deck of this terrifying craft Clarissa ruled her far-flung empire, sending bone-chilling e-mails to incompetent staff members around the world. In addition, she fired her boat's skipper, who had overslept and failed to meet Clarissa at the appointed 5 A.M. launch time, by angrily flashing him a series of semaphore signals as he watched helplessly from the pier. At the end of the day, flush with accomplishment, she steered her vessel toward land, hoping to dock at an exclusive local eatery called Snub Harbor. But when the restaurant's bouncer refused to let her drop anchor, a course of events was set into motion that would change Clarissa's life forever.

Accounts differ as to what, exactly, happened next. At her trial, Clarissa claimed that she did not steer her boat into the nightspot in a fit of rage, as eighty-two separate witnesses swore she did. To the contrary, she said she was attempting to steer her boat away from shore, but instead of pulling the lever labeled *reverse* she mistakenly pulled the one labeled *attack*. But Clarissa's doom may have been sealed by the damning testimony of the nightspot's bouncer, who testified that Clarissa went "totally bat-shit" and shouted "I'm gonna get you muthahs!" before sending the hull of her boat plowing into the restaurant. Regardless of whom you believe—and, as a fellow CEO, I tend to believe Clarissa—the results of this unfortunate incident are a matter of public record. Clarissa's boat injured scores of diners and, even worse, closed the restaurant for the remainder of August, its most lucrative month.

As police combed through the wreckage, however, a

bad situation for Clarissa grew steadily worse. Investigators discovered sensitive company documents that had been stored onboard the boat and that offered evidence of a price-fixing scheme designed to make the retail price of decoupage kits soar to unprecedented levels. In addition, they got their hands on several key pieces of documentation offering conclusive proof that Clarissa had plagiarized some of her most famous recipes from the recipe booklet that accompanies the Easy Bake Oven™. Women across America celebrated these revelations in a hideous orgy of schadenfreude, cheered on by the jackals in the tabloid press.

Clarissa's trial, which was carried live on both Court TV and the Food Network, did not go at all well for her. A botched eye job she had had done a year earlier, while making her face appear younger and far less droopy, had the unfortunate side effect of closing her tear ducts permanently. As a result, during her sentencing it was impossible for Clarissa to cry, preventing her from showing, or even faking, contrition. One month later, Clarissa started serving her sentence at the Federal Correctional Institution for Women in the town of Catscratch Fever, Georgia. This is her story, in her own words:

> When I first came to Catscratch, I was worried about how I would be treated. You hear stories about famous people being treated badly by other prisoners, and I was bracing for the worst. As it turned out, a lot of my fears were unfounded. Sure, a lot of the women here called me "Bitch," but if anybody should have been used to that it's me.

I spent many hours alone in my cell trying to think of ideas for a business I could start up in prison. By this time, I had the cell to myself because my cell mate had been taken away to the "ding wing," which is what they call the psych ward here. To make a long story short, she'd told the guards that she had seen me making Christmas ornaments and gingerbread men at 3 A.M. in the middle of July, and they assumed she was hallucinating. I was happy to see her go, so I let them believe what they wanted to believe.

It was hard to get much thinking done in my cell, because the women in the cell next to mine were always arguing into the wee hours of the morning, using language that would peel the paint off a cute wicker chaise longue that you picked up at a yard sale on Shelter Island. At first, I was going to tell them to keep it down, but then I realized: This is the idea I've been looking for.

Today, I am CEO of the fourth-largest phone sex business in America, grossing over $600 million dollars in pretax—oops, I mean, no-tax!—earnings. The market of people who want to talk to foul-mouthed female prisoners seems to be growing daily, and we haven't even made a plunge yet into the Far East, which we expect to be huge. I guess I should be worried about competitors, but I'm not. If any other women here tried to set up their own phone sex business, my "board of directors" has ways to make them stop. (These chicks even scare *me,* and that's really saying something!)

Running a company behind bars has been wonderful and gratifying, but I'd be lying if I said that I didn't still struggle with sexism sometimes. A female CEO in prison is judged differently from a male CEO—sometimes unfairly. Female CEOs who physically attack other inmates with rakes or other garden tools, for example, are criticized for being too "emotional," while a male prisoner who does the same thing is often spoken of in admiring terms for being a "bad ass." Talk about a double standard! I guess all this means is that we convicted female CEOs have come a long way in this country, but we still have a long way to go.

11

How Golden Is Your Hacksaw?
Exit Strategies

It's fitting, I suppose, that the final chapter of this book is Chapter 11. I thought I'd better point that out before some wise-ass reader did.

Anyone who has ever been through a Chapter Eleven bankruptcy reorganization knows that, while it is in some ways an ending, it is also a beginning—a fresh start. That was very much the case when Shamco went into Chapter Eleven. It marked both the ending of the company as a business that people were willing to invest in, and the beginning of a lengthy prison sentence for yours truly, thirty other top Shamco executives, seven members of our accounting firm, and the guy who watered our office plants, who was implicated in a way that I'm still a little fuzzy about.

Much like Chapter Eleven bankruptcy, this chapter is in some ways an ending and a beginning. It is an ending in that, technically speaking, it is the last chapter of this book. But it is also a beginning in that it deals with a "fresh start": the new life that a convicted CEO will embark upon when he decides that he has accomplished all that he can in prison, and that it is time for him to "move on."

There is a moment in every imprisoned CEO's career when he knows that the business he has started up behind bars is mature and can survive without him. While it may be painful to come to this realization, it's not nearly so painful as 90 percent of the other things he'll experience behind bars.

For me, this moment came three months after I started my prison jumpsuit business, Scamco. I was sitting on top of the world; our profits were sky high, our jumpsuits appeared regularly in the pages of *Women's Wear Daily,* and *People* reported that Gwyneth Paltrow intended to wear one to the upcoming Academy Awards ceremonies. And yet, as satisfying as my success was, I felt oddly— well, imprisoned by it. As I fed a ream of documents to Snake for him to chew and swallow, I thought to myself, "Do I want to be doing this ten years from now?" I'd achieved all I'd set out to achieve; I'd made my mark; I'd transferred one hundred million dollars to my bank account in Bermuda. I had to look at myself in the mirror and admit it: I wasn't having fun anymore. And if being in prison is no longer about having fun, then what's the point?

Another motivating factor in my decision to move on was a series of troubling letters I'd received from Conspicuosa. Her tennis pro, Chad, a relatively minor figure in her earlier letters to me, now seemed to be playing an increasingly prominent role in each new letter I received. Suddenly, she couldn't go a sentence without saying "Chad this" or "Chad that," which contributed to my growing sense of unease. If she was relying that much upon a barely literate tennis pro to keep her company, she must have been missing me terribly. The suffering that the Department of Justice had wreaked upon this brave but oddly vulnerable woman stung once more like a freshly reopened wound, reminding me of my first week at Lomax when Snake spanked me in the face with a shovel. I vowed to escape from the penitentiary and return to her side as quickly as possible. True, we'd be fugitives, Conspicuosa and I, forever on the road with no place to call a home. But if that sort of life was good enough for my former partner, Viktor M. Saurian, it was good enough for me—assuming, of course, that Viktor was still alive.

There will come a day when you, too, decide that the time has come for you to escape from prison, or take advantage of "fence parole," as such escapes are sometimes called. But let's remember our habit of "putting first things first." Before you break out of prison, think: "What will happen to my company when I'm gone?"

As amazing as it may seem, the typical CEO who is

planning his escape from prison often devotes hours of thought to the minutiae of punching out windows, shimmying under barbed wire, and outrunning murderous guard dogs, while devoting almost no thought whatsoever to creating an orderly succession plan so that his company can prosper in his absence. I wasn't about to make that mistake.

After evaluating my top Six Sigma "Black Belts," I chose Snake to be interim CEO, with the understanding that he would fully assume control of Scamco once I was safely beyond the prison walls. After weeks of digging, my Six Sigma team leaders successfully created a tunnel leading from under the prison cafeteria to a wooded area just outside the prison gates. By working together the Six Sigma Way, nothing could possibly go wrong. Soon, Conspicuosa and I would be together again, Chad would be toast, and a new chapter in my business life would begin—Chapter 12, I guess.

Even Six Sigma, as I learned on the night of my escape attempt, can screw up every now and then.

At first, everything went like clockwork. I had decided to time my escape to coincide with a screening of the film *Stuart Little 2* for all of the inmates in the prison cafeteria. Fifteen minutes into the movie, right on cue, Snake leapt to his feet and shouted, "This isn't as good as *Stuart Little 1!*" A carefully choreographed riot ensued, providing me with the diversion I needed to lift up four already-loosened floor tiles and drop down into the tunnel that my Six Sigma teammates had diligently prepared for my exit.

As I crawled through the narrow tunnel to freedom, I

could barely contain my excitement as I contemplated the dynamic new life that lay ahead. Just as being an indicted CEO had prepared me for being an incarcerated CEO, so had being an incarcerated CEO prepared me for being a fugitive CEO. True, I'd be hounded by law enforcement for the rest of my life, but in this age of wireless technology, being on the run was no biggie. In fact, not having an office, an address, or even a valid passport meant that I could travel lighter, move faster, and react to change better than an old-style, desk-bound CEO who wasn't wanted by the law. Yes, being a fugitive CEO was the "new new thing," and I was getting in on the ground floor.

I reached the end of the tunnel and popped my head out, ready to take the first luxurious breath of my exciting new life. But then, suddenly, I was blinded by a punishing flash of light.

Camera crews from CNN, CNBC, and all the other usual suspects were lying in wait for me, their sound trucks parked a short distance away. Three Department of Justice stooges unceremoniously yanked me from the tunnel and clasped handcuffs on my wrists in a sickening tableau of déjà vu. I was on another "perp walk," only this time they didn't have to put me on a bus to prison—they merely walked me back in. If you can think of anything more humiliating than that, I'd like to know what you've got in mind.

It was only after my interview with the warden that I pieced together what had happened. Snake, far from being a trusted second-in-command, turned out to have been a sleazebag of legendary proportions. Rather than swallowing and eating all of the documents I had been feeding him over the weeks, he had secreted the most incriminating of them in his jumpsuit, later sharing them with law enforcement in exchange for an early parole date. By his design, the evening's riot had morphed from a charade meant to spring me to a ruse guaranteed to ensnare me. Thanks to my former cell mate, Scamco went down in flames that night, and took me down with it—hard. I'd seen treachery in my business career before, but never from someone like Snake, who didn't even have an MBA. Maybe this is why so many CEOs are reluctant to name a successor.

As I said before, this chapter, Chapter 11, is about an ending, but it is also about a beginning—a new beginning.

One day after the feds moved in and shut down Scamco, they informed me that I would be moving on to a new life, although not the one I had been contemplating as I inched my way through the tunnel. They're sending me to a maximum-security facility out in California where only the toughest customers go. I'll be locked alone in a cell, segregated from the rest of the prison population, and watched by guards and surveillance cameras on a twenty-four-hour basis, seven days a week.

I guess their intent in all of this is to keep me from starting up another company. If that's their goal, I wish them luck. You can put a CEO behind bars, but you can't put bars around his brain, and mine is already working overtime.

If I can somehow convince the guards to play ball with me, possibly by making them Class B shareholders, I could use all of those surveillance cameras to convert my cell into a state-of-the-art television studio. With virtually no overhead, I could produce original prison-based reality programming that could be offered to broadcast and satellite networks around the world. It's all a matter of coming up with a business plan, and that's always been my strength. The rest is just details, and in my experience, the details usually take care of themselves. All I can say is, I'm really stoked.

———

About the Author

ANDY BOROWITZ is a humorist for *The New Yorker*,
an essayist on National Public Radio's *Weekend Edition
Sunday,* and creator of the award-winning humor site
BorowitzReport.com. He is innocent of any and all
wrongdoings and believes that in time he will be fully
exonerated.